Pebble® Bilingüe/Bilingual Plus

D0793714

Perros de trabajo/Working Dogs

Perros policías
K-9 Police Dogs

WITHDRAWN

por/by Mari Schuh

Editora consultora/Consulting Editor: Gail Saunders-Smith, PhD

Consultor/Consultant: Oficial/Officer David Dewey, Unidad K-9/K-9 Unit,
Departamento de Policía de Colchester/Colchester Police Department
Colchester, Vermont

CAPSTONE PRESS
a capstone imprint

Pebble Plus is published by Capstone Press,
1710 Roe Crest Drive, North Mankato, Minnesota 56003.
www.capstonepub.com

Books published by Capstone Press are manufactured with paper containing at least 10 percent post-consumer waste.

Library of Congress Cataloging-in-Publication Data
Schuh, Mari C., 1975–
 [K-9 police dogs. Spanish & English]
 Perros policías / por by Mari Schuh = K-9 police dogs / by Mari Schuh.
 p. cm.—(Pebble plus bilingual. Working dogs)
 Parallel text in English and Spanish.
 Includes index.
 Summary: "Simple text and full-color photos illustrate the traits, training, and duties of K-9 police dogs—in both English and Spanish"—Provided by publisher.
 ISBN 978-1-4296-6899-6 (library binding)
 1. Police dogs—Juvenile literature. I. Title. II. Title: K-9 police dogs. III. Series.
HV8025.S3918 2012
363.2—dc22   2011000648

Editorial Credits

Erika Shores, editor; Strictly Spanish, translation services; Bobbie Nuytten, designer; Danielle Ceminsky, bilingual book designer; Marcie Spence, media researcher; Laura Manthe, production specialist

Photo Credits

Capstone Studio/Karon Dubke, 1, 5, 11, 15, 19, 21
Courtesy of Officer David Dewey of Colchester Police Department, 9
Mark Raycroft, cover
Newscom, 7, 17
Shutterstock/Cherkas, 13

Note to Parents and Teachers

The Perros de trabajo/Working Dogs series supports national social studies standards related to people, places, and culture. This book describes and illustrates K-9 police dogs in both English and Spanish. The images support early readers in understanding the text. The repetition of words and phrases helps early readers learn new words. This book also introduces early readers to subject-specific vocabulary words, which are defined in the Glossary section. Early readers may need assistance to read some words and to use the Table of Contents, Glossary, Internet Sites, and Index sections of the book.

Printed in the United States of America in North Mankato, Minnesota.
022012
006603R

Table of Contents

Tabla de contenidos

Fighting Crime

Police K-9s are four-legged crime fighters. These brave dogs help the police.

Combatir el crimen

Los perros policías son luchadores del crimen con cuatro patas. Estos perros valientes ayudan a la policía.

Police dogs chase criminals.
They also search for
missing people.

Los perros policías persiguen
criminales. Ellos también
buscan personas perdidas.

Police dogs sniff for drugs and bombs. They scratch at the spot where they find drugs. They sit down where they find bombs.

Los perros policías olfatean drogas y bombas. Ellos rasguñan el lugar donde encuentran las drogas. Ellos se sientan donde encuentran bombas.

The Right Kind of Dog

Police dogs are outstanding dogs. They always follow commands. An excellent sense of smell helps them do their job.

El tipo correcto de perro

Los perros policías son perros sobresalientes. Ellos siempre siguen órdenes. Un sentido del olfato excelente los ayuda a realizar su trabajo.

Male German shepherds make good police dogs. They are strong, smart, and aggressive.

Los ovejeros alemanes machos son siempre buenos perros policías. Ellos son fuertes, inteligentes y agresivos.

K-9 police dog in training/Perro policía en entrenamiento

Training

Police dogs begin training after their first birthday. They learn commands. They search for smells and are rewarded with a toy.

Entrenamiento

Los perros policías comienzan su entrenamiento después de su primer cumpleaños. Ellos aprenden órdenes. Ellos buscan olores y son recompensados con un juguete.

On the Job

Police dogs patrol streets with police officers. These dogs climb stairs and jump over walls.

En el trabajo

Los perros policías patrullan las calles con oficiales de policía. Estos perros suben escaleras y saltan sobre paredes.

Police dogs wear vests for protection. They are called tactical vests.

Los perros policías usan chalecos de protección.
Se llaman chalecos tácticos.

Police dogs work for about six to eight years. They fight crime with the police every day.

Los perros policías trabajan entre seis y ocho años. Ellos combaten el crimen con la policía todos los días.

Glossary

aggressive—strong and forceful; male German shepherds are naturally aggressive; their police dog training keeps them from being too aggressive

command—an order to follow a direction

criminal—a person who breaks the law

patrol—to walk or travel around an area to protect it or to keep watch on people

tactical vest—a piece of equipment worn to protect people or animals during times of danger

Internet Sites

FactHound offers a safe, fun way to find Internet sites related to this book. All of the sites on FactHound have been researched by our staff.

Here's all you do:

Visit *www.facthound.com*

Type in this code: 9781429668996

 Check out projects, games and lots more at **www.capstonekids.com**

Glosario

agresivo—fuerte y energético; los ovejeros alemanes machos son naturalmente agresivos; el entrenamiento con la policía evita que sean demasiado agresivos

el chaleco táctico—una pieza de equipo usada para proteger personas o animales durante periodos de peligro

el criminal—una persona que quebranta la ley

la orden—comando para seguir una instrucción

patrullar—caminar o viajar alrededor de un área para protegerla o vigilar a personas

Sitios de Internet

FactHound brinda una forma segura y divertida de encontrar sitios de Internet relacionados con este libro. Todos los sitios en FactHound han sido investigados por nuestro personal.

Esto es todo lo que tienes que hacer:

Visita *www.facthound.com*

Ingresa este código: 9781429668996

¡Algo súper divertido! Hay proyectos, juegos y mucho más en www.capstonekids.com

Index

Índice